American Symbols

The Pledge of Allegiance

By Lloyd G. Douglas

SCHOLASTIC INC.

New York Toronto London Auckland Sydney
Mexico City New Delhi Hong Kong Buenos Aires

Photo Credits: Cover © Steve Chenn/Corbis; pp. 7, 17, 21 (bottom left) © Bettmann/Corbis; p. 9 © Joseph Sohm; ChromoSohm Inc./Corbis; pp. 11, 21 (top left) © Nathan Benn/Corbis; pp. 13, 15, 21 (top right) © Eyewire; pp. 19, 21 (bottom right) © Bruce Burkhardt/Corbis
Contributing Editor: Jennifer Silate
Book Design: Christopher Logan

ISBN 0-516-24486-8

12 11 10 9 8 7 6 5 4 3 2 1   3 4 5 6 7 8/0

Printed in the U.S.A.   61

First Scholastic paperback printing, September 2003

Contents

The **Pledge of Allegiance** is an American **symbol**.

It is a promise Americans make to **support** the United States of America.

I pledge allegiance to the flag
of the United States of America
and to the republic for which it stands,
one nation under God, indivisible,
with liberty and justice for all.

People have been saying the Pledge of Allegiance for more than one hundred years.

7

Today, people put their right hand over their heart when they say the Pledge of Allegiance.

People also look at the American **flag** when they say the Pledge of Allegiance.

The American flag stands for the United States of America.

13

There are fifty stars on the American flag.

Each star stands for a state.

15

We promise **liberty** and **justice** for everyone in the Pledge of Allegiance.

People in America say the Pledge of Allegiance in schools and many other places.

The Pledge of Allegiance is a promise that Americans make to their country.

It is a symbol of America.

21

New Words

flag (**flag**) a piece of cloth that has different shapes
and colors on it

justice (**juhss**-tiss) fair treatment

liberty (**lib**-ur-tee) freedom

Pledge of Allegiance (**plej uhv** uh-**lee**-junss)
a promise that people make to the United States

support (suh-**port**) to believe in or help something

symbol (**sim**-buhl) an object that represents
something else

To Find Out More

Web Site
The Story and Meaning of the Pledge of Allegiance
http://www.flagday.org/Pages/StoryofPledge.html
This Web site explains the meaning of the Pledge of Allegiance
and tells its history.

Index

About the Author
Lloyd G. Douglas is an editor and writer of children's books.

Reading Consultants
Kris Flynn, Coordinator, Small School District Literacy, The San Diego County
Office of Education

Shelly Forys, Certified Reading Recovery Specialist, W.J. Zahnow Elementary
School, Waterloo, IL

Sue McAdams, Former President of the North Texas Reading Council of the
IRA, and Early Literacy Consultant, Dallas, TX